Calligraphy Techniques

Mary Noble

ABBEYDALE PRESS

INTRODUCTION

Observers who know that I am a calligrapher are shocked to find how untidy my everyday note-taking is. I use a ballpoint pen like most people, and as long as I can read what I have written, that's fine by me.

When writing to a friend, I tend to take more care, keen that my writing should both be readable and look good on the page. I sometimes choose a narrow fibre-tip pen as it has more 'drag' than a ballpoint, and makes me write more slowly.

When it comes to calligraphy, that's slower still. Now I take great care with every letter, using a broad-edged pen and striving to make all the letters look as if they belong to a matching set – almost as if they were part of a type font. But not so much like a font that I might as well type the letter out on the computer! Indeed, there are fonts available that exploit that 'hand-made' look so cleverly that sometimes you are not sure of their origin; if they are very beautiful, then you can be sure that they were designed or adapted from a hand-drawn original.

The attraction of using calligraphy is that it allows us to produce something that both looks beautiful, and proclaims itself to be hand-made. There is a definite sensual pleasure for the writer in making rhythmical movements with a pen; the fact that these marks represent words gives us the motivation to use the technique frequently. For the reader, the pleasure is in appreciating the beauty of the completed work. And in between those two, as I know from

teaching my classes, lies the fascination of the performance, of watching a calligrapher write!

Try it for yourself. Accept the fact that you will not become expert in a couple of weeks. As with all skills, you need to practise regularly, and to develop an eye for accuracy. Stick with one alphabet style until you can reproduce it without constant reference to a book, before you try another. Never get stuck on one letter – give it three attempts, then move on to other letters and come back to it later. The experience of creating the other letters will help you to shape that first one again, but this time better.

Practising is important, but employing calligraphy to make something is better still. That way you get to practise while you also create an end product. The motivation of having to prepare, for instance, some labels for a friend will encourage you to finish the job, when otherwise you might have let the whole project slide.

So, ignore the scruffiness of your note-taking – and mine too – and resolve to accept calligraphy as a separate branch of writing; one that's slower, more graceful, and more carefully crafted. It is writing for special occasions, to be enjoyed both by the writer and the reader alike.

Through & through

GREAT POWER IS OURS

such that all Creation,
in all things, stands by us

THE EARTH
should not be injured

THE EARTH
should not be destroyed

HILDEGARDE *of* BINGHAM

LEFT-HANDERS

Approximately one in ten people write using their left hand,
while some of them have learned to write with both hands
because they were persuaded against their natural inclination
in their early years.

Western left-handers have had it
tough ever since the Romans took to
writing from left to right; a direction
which favours the right-hander.

The Greeks wrote 'boustrophedon'
style, left to right then right to left
like ploughing a field (the Greek
literally means 'like an ox turning').
Chinese characters are written in
vertical columns from right to left,
and ancient Egyptians wrote in any
direction that took their fancy.

Right-handers generally hold their pens with the handle
pointing towards the elbow (see below), and move the
right hand across the body to start on the left. As they
write, they can see what has been written and the pen is
generally pulled across or towards the body. Letter strokes
usually go from top to bottom, or left to right.

A left-hander doing the same thing has to twist his or
her wrist to hold the pen at the same angle.

If, instead, the left-hander chooses to hold the pen at a
more comfortable angle – in a mirror image of a right-
hander – most strokes will have to be pushed rather than
pulled, and there is a constant hazard of smudging what
has just been written. It would be more natural for a left-
hander to write from right to left.

Many left-handers write with their hand hooked over, which works well with a pointed instrument, but this is not so easy when using a broad-edged pen, because the thicks and thins can occur in the wrong places, and smudging is again a hazard.

One solution, which some left-handed 'hook' calligraphers use very successfully, is to write from the bottom up – in effect following all those directional arrows on exemplars in reverse. Indeed, some people start from the right, pull up from the base, and spell backwards!

There are disadvantages, however: you are not reproducing the stroke order and direction used in the original models, for example with the upward flick of an Italic exit stroke. Thus you will not create the less formal, freer letterforms accurately because you are doing them backwards.

If you are left-handed, and you don't follow the 'hook' method (see picture above right), then some minor adjustments are all you need to write with an edged pen for calligraphy:

• Place your paper to your left, not directly in front of you, and get into the habit of moving the paper in that direction so that your hand never has to come across your body.

• Sit facing slightly to the left of your work.

• Note where your elbow is; tuck it against your side; if it sticks out, you will have to twist your wrist uncomfortably.

• Write on a raised board, so you have a better view of the area where you are writing.

Some manufacturers provide left-oblique nibs (see picture right) to help left-handers, so you don't have to twist so far. It is worth investigating what is available locally. However, the selection will inevitably be smaller, because the market is at maximum only 10 per cent of practising calligraphers.

Filing nibs to the required angle often makes them too sharp, or uneven, unless you are well practised in this technique.

You may prefer to develop the above strategies in order to be able to make full use of all the various pens manufactured for the majority of right-handers. Just remember to blame the Romans!

RULING LINES

In order to keep a consistency of writing height, and to keep your lines straight, ruling accurate lines is really important. There are several ways to achieve this, but in every case a sharp pencil and accurate measuring are the keys to success.

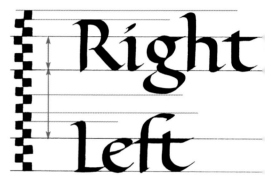

HOW WIDE?

First you need to know how far apart to rule your lines, so start with the pen you plan to use, and the alphabet style you want to write. Every alphabet style has its own standard measurement, called 'nib-widths', which is the number of times the width of the nib fits into the height of the main part of the letter. (This is shown with each alphabet exemplar.) That means, whether you write with a big or small pen nib, the letters will look the same scale.

Foundational hand is four nib-widths high, so hold your pen sideways and make squares like these, just touching. You can do either a 'ladder' or a 'staircase', but try to avoid the pitfalls shown here:

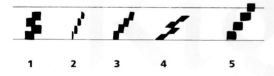

1   **2**   **3**   **4**   **5**

1 Overlapping – check the white spaces to see if they are the width of your pen.

2 These marks are too tentative to serve as accurate measurements.

3 Overlapping in the staircase method; this is the same problem as 1 but not so easy to spot at small sizes.

4 Wrong pen angle – you really have to work at it to get a totally vertical pen angle.

5 Even tiny gaps compound to make a big error.

HOW MANY LINES DO I NEED?

This is where confusion can develop on a grand scale – only rule the most essential lines. Here are ruled the 'body' or 'x' height lines, but you can see that if you wanted them, you could also add lines for capitals, ascenders and descenders. Don't do it! Experience shows that the more lines you rule, the greater is the chance of writing on the wrong ones! Instead, train your eye to estimate accurately, noticing the following: there always has to be a clearance gap between descenders on one line and ascenders on the next. Ascenders in most alphabets are a little bit taller than the capitals. Capitals are often two nib-widths taller than the body height.

✔ ✗ ✗ ✗

1 **2** **3** **4**

RULING THE LINES

If you have the equipment, the ideal method for speed is to mark the measurements down one side of the page, secure the page to a board, and use a T-square to rule parallel lines.

SERIFS

Writing between the lines usually means starting just below, and finishing with a leading-out stroke just above them. These little sideways movements create neat pointed beginnings and ends to letters – serifs – that would otherwise have blunt ends. Make sure you do them without too much over-emphasis.

1 A Foundational 'i' with serifs that are a small proportion of the whole stroke.

2 Blunt ends – not enough of a thin edge of the pen used.

3 Too much serif, so it starts and ends thick instead of thin.

4 This letter is all serif – it is over-emphasized to the extent of losing the letterform.

If you only have a ruler, mark the measurements carefully down both sides of the page and rule across. Do a spot check by measuring a few lines across the centre to see that they are accurate.

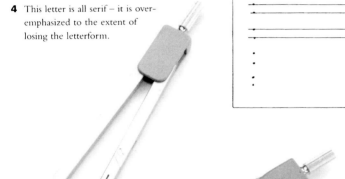

Another method is to mark the measurements on a strip of paper and then transfer these to both edges of the paper and rule across as before. This method will not be as accurate and is not recommended when working at small sizes.

Some people use a pair of dividers (which are like a compass but with two points) pricking the same measurement all the way down the page. Then you rule lines leaving out the one which allows for the double gap.

ROMAN CAPITALS

ROMAN CAPITALS are the foundation stones of our Western writing. Their forms have survived for 2000 years, despite the attractions of many other scripts which have developed since Roman times. While you may feel familiar with the main shapes, for calligraphy you need to take note of the subtleties of their widths and proportions, which the Romans perfected, in order to make them beautiful.

The subtlety of these forms is largely determined by how each letter relates to a square or a circle. Here they are shown in related width groups.

NIB-WIDTHS

The standard weight for Roman Capitals uses seven nib-widths and a pen angle of 30° from the horizontal. This angle is just enough to make the horizontal strokes thinner than the vertical strokes – best illustrated in the letters H and T. If all your strokes are same thickness, you are using a 45° pen angle, which is a common mistake.

BPRK
SELFIJ

THE HALF-WIDTH GROUP

The main portion of these letters fills half the square – but the leg of R and K sticks out a little. Note how the mid-point join in B, P and R varies in each case – B's join comes above halfway, while P is on or just below and R is definitely below that point. K is just above. This creates visual stability. The cross-bars of E and F sit on the mid-point.

HNTU
AVXYZ

THE THREE-QUARTER WIDTH GROUP

Actually, it's not exactly three-quarters – it's the width you establish when the diagonals of the square intersect with the circumference of the circle. If you have trouble gauging their width in the early stages, mark the correct width on a scrap of paper and hold it over each letter after you have made it.

Compare the upright strokes in H and N; N's uprights are inscribed at a steeper angle (60°) to provide a contrast with the thick diagonal.

CDGOQ

THE CIRCULAR GROUP

Based on a complete circle, these letters are difficult to write at first as we tend to make them narrower than they should be. Note how little of the circle is missing from C, D and G. The cross-bar of G rises to about halfway up the vertical scale.

MW

THE SQUARE GROUP

Strictly speaking, M is the only letter in this group! W is actually wider than the square, by half a 'V'; turn the book upside down and you will see that these letters are not upside-down versions of one another.

A B C D E
F G H I J K
L M N O P
Q R S T U
V W X Y Z

COMMON MISTAKES

B E D G M R S V

1   2   3   4   5   6   7   8

1 B is top-heavy.

2 The centre stroke is too short, while the others are too long in this E.

3 Make D occupy more of the circle.

4 Raise the cross-bar in G approximately to the centre.

5 This is an upside-down W! For an M, straighten its legs.

6 Note the ugly bunching effect at the centre of the R.

7 Flatten the ends of S.

8 The pen angle has turned which makes the second stroke in V too thin

SPACING: LETTERS, WORDS AND LINES

1 Capitals need careful spacing if they are to maintain their elegance. The word 'BILL' features several upright strokes which have been positioned close together; unfortunately, no matter how closely you put the two L's, there will always be a larger space between them than exists between the I and the L. Similarly in 'LAWYER' – all the letters here are placed close together, creating uneven gaps between them.
2 When you want to check your spacing, look at it upside-down; now

¹ LAWYER BILL

² ꓶꓶꓮꓶ ꓤ∃⅄ꟽⱯꓶ

₃ LAWYER BILL

the gaps are more noticeable. It helps to mark in with a pencil where you want to increase or decrease space.
3 This is better spacing; keep the L and A as close as you can, as they already have lots of their own space, move W farther away, keep Y close, and so on.

The End

COMBINING CAPITALS WITH LOWER-CASE

The Roman Capital will not look out of place with any other letterform, but its most usual lower-case companion is the Foundational Hand. If you are using capitals within mainly lower case text, then your lines should be ruled for lower-case spacing only. Gauge the height of the capitals by eye; they should be lower than the ascenders.

---

¹ AND WHERE 'TIS FINE
IT SENDS SOME PRECI
AFTER THE THING IT LO

² AND WHERE 'TIS FINE
IT SENDS SOME PRECI
AFTER THE THING IT L

³ AND WHERE
TIS FINE IT SEN
SOME PRECIOUS
INSTANCE OF
ITSELF AFTER TH

SPACING LINES

When you are writing entirely in capitals, it is fun to experiment with the spaces between lines. The standard gap is the same height as the letters themselves (**1**); this aids readability, particularly in long lines of text.

If you want a closer texture to your design, try line spaces set at half the height of your letters (**2**); this spacing is standard for contemporary designs.

If readability is less important than getting a block of texture, or if you are using only one or two words per line, try writing with no gaps (**3**); make sure that you leave only minimal spaces between words or you will find big white gaps within your texture.

VARIATIONS

Once you have grasped the fundamentals of Roman Capitals, all sorts of possibilities for playing with the basic forms present themselves. Try copying some of these examples shown on the opposite page.

A Heavy (three nib-widths) and densely packed for impact.
B Double stroke – the second stroke is added with the same pen held sideways.
C Small, wide and spread out laterally.
D Chunky, with slab serifs, written on rougher paper to give texture to the letters.
E Lightweight, about 14 nib-widths high.
F Manipulated – the pen is twisted to achieve thicker and thinner strokes.
G Free – written quickly with a ruling pen.

A

B MN

C SHAKESPEARE

D ABCDE

E SHAKESP

F MANIPUL

G

THE FOUNDATIONAL HAND

THIS SCRIPT, or 'hand', is the one most frequently used as a teaching hand for beginners, hence its title. It is plain, unadorned, and easy to read. Edward Johnston, the father of the modern revival in calligraphy in the early 1900s, gave it this name when he designed it, using as his inspiration a particularly beautiful, classic hand in a tenth-century English manuscript, the Ramsay Psalter (now in the British Library, London).

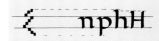

NIB-WIDTHS

Rule lines at four nib-widths high for the body of the letter. Note the heights of ascenders, descenders and capitals, but do not rule all these lines! Use your eye to judge. Just rule 'tramlines' for the body height, and set these tramlines twice the body height apart. The pen angle should be approximately 30° from the horizontal.

It is written fairly slowly, with several strokes to each letter; note how the shapes of the letters 'a' and 'g' are much more familiar to us as type than as handwriting.

This is a popular hand for formal projects, and occasions which demand plain text.

Use the Roman Capitals with this hand.

ocepqbd g s

nmhar u lt ɪjk

vwxyz n a t e

LETTER SHAPES

Try copying the letters that are most similar to each other in groups, as shown. Note particularly the 'o' shaped letters and the arched ('m', 'n' etc.) letters.

The letter O is the governing shape for most of the alphabet, so make sure you think of O when you write; if you do, the arch in 'n' will

join very high up, and the bottom shape of 'a' will be in line with its 'roof', and 'e' will not be too narrow – these are all common errors to avoid.

a b c d e f g

h i j k l m n

o p q r s t u

v w x y z &

COMMON MISTAKES

a d s e n n r g

1   2   3   4   5   6   7   8

1 Keep the 'roof' of 'a' as wide as the base; the top stroke should be the same as in 'n'.

2 Flatten the top curve in the bowl of 'd' to avoid too much thickness.

3 Open out the white shapes to make it more rounded – flatten top and bottom end strokes.

4 Wrong angle, give 'e' more curve and flatten the angle of the thin stroke.

5 Arch starts too low, giving it a weak join.

6 Good arch, but a weak serif at the starting stroke.

7 Make the 'r' stroke as you would when starting an 'n'.

8 Don't forget the final top stroke; this is an elegant tail, but you may not have room for this much in general usage.

SPACING LETTERS

Some letters come with space attached to them, like 't', 'r' and 'a'; take pity on those which don't, like 'i' and 'n', and be generous on their behalf. Look what happens if you don't – in the top line 'r' and 'a' together pool their space and make it enormous, while next door the 'n's' and 'i's' are closely packed. You need to even out the spaces by packing 'r' and 'a' close together and spreading out the others.

training

training

LINE SPACING

The standard gap between lines for the Foundational hand is twice its body height. This leaves plenty of clearance for the ascenders and descenders; it also allows the eye to travel comfortably along lines of text, so you could write ten-word lines without impairing readability.

For short designs it is sometimes necessary to reduce the space between lines of writing, but beware of potential clashes between ascenders and descenders, and keep the lines short.

every landscape here
we find to be more
beautiful than the

every landscape
we find to be

VARIATIONS

When you are thoroughly familiar with the Foundational hand, you could try copying a few of these variations shown on the opposite page:

1 Lightweight: write it with more nib-widths than the norm; this takes a steady hand.
2 Written using an automatic pen, with a flick of the edge of the nib for lightweight serifs.
3 Contrasting light and heavy weights; this works best if the words are pushed close together.

4 Compressing laterally (and with a second colour dropped in while wet).
5 Chunky letters with wedge serifs to create a sturdy look.
6 Lightweight and expanded (and with a colour change).
7 Tall and squashed: take care not to let it become italic.

1 abcdefg

2 n

3 greetings
greetings
greetings
greetings
greetings

4 alphabet

5 abcdefghij

6 extension

7 extension

THE UNCIAL HAND

THE UNCIAL hand is a complete alphabet on its own, having no separate lower-case form. It looks rather like an alphabet that has not quite made up its mind whether to be capital (majuscule) or lower-case (minuscule). This is because of its ancestry, dating as it does from about the seventh century when many influences were at work.

NIB-WIDTHS
Usually work at four nib-widths, but you could try three and a half or even three for heavier effects. The pen angle is flatter than for most other styles, 15° or 20° from the horizontal.

There are many versions of Uncials, but this one is comfortable in pen angle and has a contemporary look. Use it for less formal work, titles, and where you want bold text. It is particularly effective in small sizes as the simple shapes remain very readable.

LETTER SHAPES
The round 'o' shape governs the form of most letters, so ensure you keep your letters wide, especially these shown which often become narrower by mistake.

LETTER HEIGHT
Some of the letters, although they are capitals, emerge slightly above or below the guidelines (body height). This is history's first sign of a developing lower-case. Keep them absolutely minimal.

LETTER SPACING
Try to even out the spaces between letters, using your eye to judge what looks balanced. The first example is clearly unbalanced, as straight shapes can be pushed more closely together than curves. The T in this form has all that space in front, so push the following letter as close as possible next to it.

The second example shows more even spreading; those letters which do not come with their own space already attached (N, I,) need your help to give them the room they need. Others need their space limiting (R, E, T). If you are uncertain if you have it right or not, view the word upside down.

COMMON MISTAKES

1 Over-emphasis on the top curve and a small bowl shape make this 'a' unbalanced.
2 The top of 'd' is sagging downwards; give it a lift.
3 This 'e' is too narrow.
4 Too narrow and forward sloping.
5 Both sides of the 'm' should be rounded.
6 Twist the pen to get thinner upright strokes, and put more 'bounce' into the letter!
7 Too narrow – the bowl should be more open.

LINE SPACING

The Uncial hand can be treated as a capital form and given less space between lines of writing because of the minimal protrusions above or below the lines. (But ensure you do keep the protrusions thus.) Here compare the overall density of the block of text written with different amounts of space between the lines.

Take care, especially when choosing closer line-spacing, that the gaps between words do not end up similar in size to the gaps between lines; if they do, the eye will have trouble travelling along the lines of text, and you will create 'rivers' of white space down the page.

ΛΝΌ SτιLL I RETURN LIKE Λ LINE το τhe CENTRE, LIKE FIRE το

ΛΝΌ SτιLL I RETURN LIKE Λ LINE το τhe CENTRE, LIKE FIRE το

ΛΝΌ SτιLL I RETURN LIKE Λ LINE το τhe CENTRE, LIKE FIRE το τhe SUN, ΛΝΌ τhe STREΛM το τhe SEΛ

VARIATIONS

Opposite are some variations that you could try:

1 Flat pen angle – horizontal – with pen twists for the serifs in 'e' and 'f'.
2 Shallow and laterally spread.
3 Contrasts in weight work well in this hand because of the lack of ascenders and descenders.
4 Lightweight – about ten nib-widths.
5 Write a block of text at three or fewer nib-widths for an overall dense texture.
6 A big chunky 'a' written with an automatic pen and a colour change.
7 Lightweight, compressed, and written with speed for liveliness.
8 As in **7**, but freely written with a ruling pen.

1 ABCD EFGh

2 wide

3 is loving and FRIDAYS works hard

4 ABCDEFG

5 the quick BROWN FOX jumps over the lazy dog

6 A

7 ABCDEFG

8 marianne

FORMAL ITALIC LOWER CASE

THE ITALIANS developed this hand in the fifteenth century during the Renaissance. They looked at tenth-century Carolingian styles for inspiration, and developed their own version, elliptical and sloping.

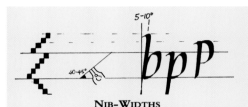

NIB-WIDTHS

Rule lines for a gap of five nib-widths, and make the ascenders and descenders just a little less than the body height, i.e. four nib-widths. The pen angle should be about 40°, and the letters slope forward by 5° to 10°.

This is the most popular calligraphic hand today, on account of its readability, flowing quality and its adaptability for variation.

Use this form with Italic or Roman Capitals. Formal Italic suits many uses, from memorial books to poetry and expressive works.

LETTER SHAPES

See how closely related the letters above are in shape to one another; the 'a' shape is reflected in 'd', 'g', 'q', 'u', and 'y'. Turn the 'a' upside down and you have the underlying shape for 'b', 'h', 'm', 'n', 'p' and 'r'. The letters which most closely relate to the 'o' are 'e' and 'c', but you can see the affinity to the other 'a' and 'b' shapes.

CRITICAL SHAPES

The 'down-and-up' structure of 'a' (right) is a critical shape to master; it is important to take the stroke right back up to the line, and not to stop near the base as in the third example here. Try it first with a pencil; the pushing movement required may feel alien at first with the edged pen.

ARCHES

This is an exercise in arches. The first 'n' (top left) shows how to keep the pen on the page and write the whole letter in one go, but it branches out too low. Aim for the second version, where the branching arch emerges about halfway up the upright. The third example still branches, but emerges rather higher up than usually desirable. The last is not italic, and is to be avoided at all costs! It has been made without the 'branching' and by taking the pen off the paper to start anew at the top, which makes a Foundational-type arch.

a b c d e f f

g h i j k l m n

o p q r s t u v

w x y y z !?&

COMMON MISTAKES

a a b m r s g e o

1   2   3   4   5   6   7   8   9

1   The pen stopped at the bottom instead of travelling right up to the top of the letter.
2   Make a corner at the top rather than a curve.
3   The ascender could be taller.
4   These arches are Foundational, not Italic; 'm' should be written without taking the pen off the page, so the arches should look 'branching' not 'stuck on'.
5   The hook at the end does not match the other letters; keep it a gentle curve.
6   Flatten the top and bottom of the 's'.
7   Flatten the bottom curve of the 'g' to avoid this stroke becoming the most dominant.
8   Divide 'e' nearer the top.
9   An uneven 'o'; this is the hardest letter to balance.

LETTER SPACING

Take care to think ahead as you write, to imagine how much space you will need between each letter as you write it. The first 'rv' are too far apart and the letters create a large inner gap – tuck them together. Double 't' and 'ft' can share a cross-bar.

The first example (right) shows uneven letter spacing; compare the space between 'z' and 'y', and between 'm' and 'e'. You should aim for an evenness between upright strokes, so spread 'm' from 'e', and tuck 'y' into 'z' to fill some of the space.

rv rv tt ft

enzymes

enzymes

LINE SPACING

The standard gap between lines of text for Italic is double spacing, i.e. twice the body height of the text. This allows for ascenders and descenders to fit without clashing, and helps readability.

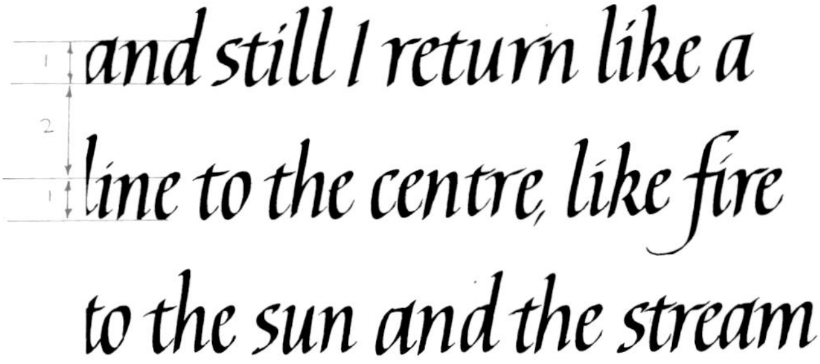

Sometimes if a closer texture is needed for your design, to give a denser overall appearance, you can write single-spaced (right). Take care with clashes, and check that you are keeping the elliptical nature of the hand; if the writing becomes too rounded, you will introduce more white into the page and you will need the extra gap between the lines to help legibility.

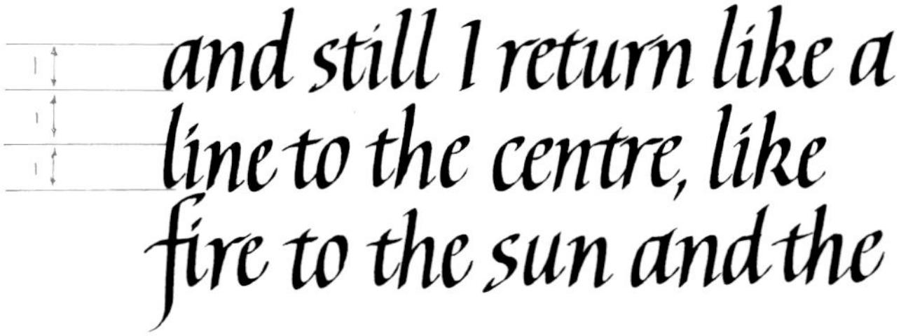

and still I return like a line to the centre, like fire to the sun and the stream

and still I return like a line to the centre, like fire to the sun and the

please close the door

On occasions when very few words are being used, they can benefit from clustering to give the overall shape greater impact to attract the eye.

VARIATIONS

Once you have practised the letter forms, try some of the variations shown opposite:

1. Automatic pen; twisted from flat to 45°.

2 Lightweight – about ten nib-widths high.

3 Shallow and laterally spread.
4 Playing with the axis.
5 Closely packed for a solid effect.
6 An alternative style of ascender.
7 Solid writing at four nib-widths.
8 Two weights of manipulated pen writing showing changes of angle.

1 *mn*

2 *light*

3 *collaboration*

4 *damp*

5 *dense pressure solid*

6 *bright light*

8 *a*

7 *heavy*

abcd

ITALIC CAPITALS

ITALIC CAPITALS are based on classical Roman Capitals, but they are compressed and sloped in order to complement the lower-case Formal Italic. They evolved during the twentieth century with the revival of interest in the italic hand as a calligraphic form; previously the Italian writing masters used versions of the Roman Capitals. Your understanding of these capitals will be greater, and you will write them more easily, if you already have some knowledge of the proportions of Roman Capitals.

NIB-WIDTHS

Seven nib-widths are commonly used, although eight will provide slightly more slender and elegant versions. The pen angle varies occasionally, but on average it is 40° from the horizontal. The letters have a slight slope, usually about 5° from the vertical, but it is acceptable to have a steeper slope (but don't vary the slope in one piece of work!). The effect of 40° plus the slope means that the horizontal strokes are thinner than the vertical ones, which produces a subtler effect than if all strokes were the same thickness.

ROMAN COMPARISONS

Compare the Roman letter O with the Italic form, and you will see what a difference compression and slope makes. The Italic version is approximately one-third narrower than the Roman. Roman Capital letters conform to several width groups; with compression, the difference between the Italic groups is less obvious, and both the wide group (such as O) and the three-quarter group (such as N) occupy the same width. Half-width letters become just a bit narrower than the others.

FITTING CAPITALS WITH LOWER CASE

If you are writing mainly in lower case, then only rule lines for the lower-case letters (see below), and use your eye to judge the capital height. The ascenders of the lower case letters should extend higher than the capital itself.

'UPLIFT'

When you write with a slope in Italic Capitals, take note of what you are doing with the horizontal strokes. They should stay parallel to the writing line, or they may be slightly raised. If they point downwards, they give your letters a depressed look. Go for uplift! Even the curved letters, like B and D, can be given slight uplift on their top curves.

A B C D E F G
H I J K L M N
O P Q R S T
U V W X Y Z

COMMON MISTAKES

B E M S R A H

1   2   3   4   5   6   7

1 Make the join of the B higher up.

2 This E is too wide at the top and bottom, and it would be improved by a serif at the top left.

3 M is unbalanced; look at the shapes created between the two uprights.

4 The S is top-heavy; look at it upside-down – much better!

5 R's leg is set too low down and is too heavy.

6 The cross-bar on A could be lower.

7 Put serifs on the H to give it subtlety.

WHEN WE TRY TO PICK

OUT ANYTHING BY ITS

WE FIND IT HITCHED

WHEN WE TRY TO PICK

OUT ANYTHING BY ITS

ELF WE FIND IT HITCH

WRITING ALL IN CAPITALS

When you are writing a whole line or more in capitals, it is essential to establish a top line to stop heights drifting. For a block of text like this (above) written all in capitals, you can experiment with the inter-line spacing. First try its own height as the space; this gives plenty of room for the eye to follow the line, even a very long one, without confusion. For a denser effect, it is better if the lines are not too long; try an inter-line space of half the line height.

LIGHTWEIGHT, TEXTURAL

If you are more interested in a textural effect and not so much in the readability, try writing with no inter-line spaces. In this example above, a lighter weight (more nib-widths) has been used.

VARIATIONS

Italic capitals lend themselves to playful variety; here are some examples shown opposite.

1 Heavy weight – about five nib-widths high.

2 Tall and narrow – a block of text with no interline space can be effective.

3 Manipulated pen – difficult at first, you twist the pen as you move down the stroke.

4 Written at speed, and with the pen well-loaded with ink.

5 More pen manipulation, this time twisting several ways.

6 Double stroke; the second thinner stroke is made with the pen held sideways in a flicking motion.

7 Pointed, with exaggerated serifs, written at speed.

1

SOLIDITY
STRENGTH
POWER

2

ABCDEF
GHIJK
LMNO
PQRST

3

POINTED

4

HURRY HURRY HURRY

5

LMN OPQR

6

WHISPER

7

SCRATCHING

NUMBERS

ROMAN NUMERALS were in common usage in Europe until at least the fifteenth century, and are still used occasionally when writing classical works. The Arabic figures that we now use took many centuries to be accepted, as the Roman heritage was very strong.

The first evidence of their arrival in Europe occurs in eleventh century. When the system finally took hold in Europe, it was found to be a much more efficient concept of counting and notation, yet Britain did not adopt Arabic numerals until the seventeenth century. We are today experiencing a similar conflict with regard to units of measurement, resulting in parallel usage of the Imperial (yes, still a Roman heritage) and metric systems.

NIB-WIDTHS
The basic model is written at a 30° pen angle and, if written with Roman Capitals, it matches their height of seven nib-widths. In contrast, the up-and-down version also shown is another popular device, generally designed to accompany lower-case lettering, as the effect is of having ascenders and descenders.

The script style in which you are writing generally determines the weight, pen angle and slope of any numbers used, but there are some general principles to apply. The basic upright, capital-height version can be taken as the standard model that would be acceptable in use with any script. The other versions are optional extras.

OTHER CHARACTERS
The $ or £ signs count as capitals, and you will find if you examine price lists in printed catalogues that the full-height version fits most needs – which caught your eye in these examples first?

THIS IS THE STANDARD USAGE
The numbers are the same height as the capitals.

THE 'LOWER-CASE' OPTION
When these numbers are used with minuscules, they generally look comfortable together because of their appearance of having ascenders and descenders. But it is just as correct to use numerals which ascend to capital height with these letters.

COMBINING NUMBERS WITH ITALIC
Experiment to decide whether the numbers you want to use look best at their full height or in the 'lower-case' version. Note that here they are sloped and compressed to match the Italic style.

EXEMPLAR

A Standard version, usually used to match capital height.

B This version is frequently favoured when combined with lower-case text.

C Italic form; sloped and compressed. You could slope and compress the above version also.

A

1 2 3 4 5

6 7 8 9 0

B

1 2 3 4 5

6 7 8 9 0

C

1 2 3 4 5

6 7 8 9 0

COMMON MISTAKES

2 4 5 6 6 8 9

1 2 3 4 5 6 7

1 Keep the top in line with the base.
2 Beware of making the cross-bar too low.
3 Out of proportion – move the bowl lower.
4 The top fades out to nothing.

5 The bowl is rather small.
6 This 8 is top-heavy – look at it upside-down to confirm this.
7 The bottom tails off with a weak ending.

BE A SCRIPT DETECTIVE

CALLIGRAPHERS SOMETIMES want to reproduce a script they have not used before, and which is not in their calligraphy books. Perhaps you need to write names in a memorial book to match the previous scribe's style. Or you see a style you like in an advertisement or another calligrapher's work. If you know how to analyse it, you can work out how to produce a complete alphabet from a small example.

Analysis is a valuable skill to develop. Calligraphers who provide alphabet exemplars generally use it to research into photographs of historic manuscripts to check the authenticity of particular details. When you become familiar with a few scripts, you may feel that you want to do the same, and to make your own decisions. The skills of analysis will help. Here is how to sift through the clues.

Find as much as you can of the script you want to study; it is unlikely that you will find every letter if you only have a few lines to work with, but even that much will suffice, with detective work. If the sample you have is only a few millimetres high, get it enlarged on a photocopier. Whatever the size, if you do not want to deface the sample you have, take a copy to work on.

The pen nib tried indicates a weight of four nib-widths; try it yourself to see if you agree.

Rule some lines and copy an 'o' – it is oval and slightly forward-sloping, perhaps made in one sweep? Then try some other o-shaped letters. If you have experience of several alphabets, you may notice that this seems to have some Uncial letterforms but Italic arches.

Make a note of the relative length of ascenders and descenders – about two-thirds the body height? Copy a few examples.

Look at the arch formation; slightly italic, but emerging high up; this indicates a pen twist to get that thin part emerging from a smooth curve. Try 'm', 'n', 'h' and other similar shapes.

Speed: fairly swift, especially the upward flicks on 'g' and 'o'.

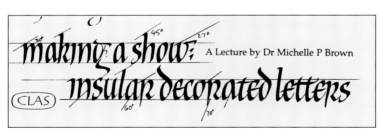

A Lecture by Dr Michelle P Brown

Try analysing the script on this invitation slip; here a photocopy has been made for experimentation purposes, so that the original does not have to be defaced.

Rule top and bottom lines – they are close together, but that is because they are part of a title; there would be some problems with clashing if this space was used all the time. Mark the angles at some entry and exit strokes – they vary a lot, and there seems to be some pen twisting going on to achieve the thin bottom of the 'r', and the thin arches on 'm' and 'n'.

Time to assemble all the letters we have; leave a mark to indicate any missing ones.

bb ff

ppqq

vv xx

yy zz

Based on the information you already have, try making up the missing letters. Should 'b' have a curved base? This might fit best with other curved letters.

The 'f' presents a quandary; there are some Uncial-type letter shapes ('d', 'g' and 'r') so perhaps the 'f' should follow suit. If you were unaware of the Uncial connection though, an italic form might occur to you, but with a pointed base like 'r', and a top like 'e'. Continue this way to create the rest of the alphabet. This method will work with any script, modern or historical. Close observation is the most important factor; if there are several examples of any letter but they all differ, select the one you consider to be the best. Experience will help you develop an eye for this.

The Flourishing Scribes Lecture   CLAS AGM SATURDAY 25TH MARCH 2PM

making a show: A Lecture by Dr Michelle P Brown
insular decorated letters

(CLAS)

FOLLOW THIS EIGHT-STAGE PLAN:

1 Rule in the lines accurately at the top and bottom of the 'x' height (body height). The first thing you can find out is how much space there is between body heights – often double, sometimes only one or one and a half, occasionally three times the body height. Note this down. This is called the 'interline space'.

2 Now try to decide what pen angle has been used; obtain an average measurement by marking lines with a ruler along several of the entry and exit strokes. Then use a protractor to read off a measurement in degrees.

3 Boldness/lightness: if it looks bold, there will be a small number of 'nib-widths', if it looks lightweight, there will be more. To find out, go through your pens and find one that matches in size – hold it over a thick stroke, perhaps in an 's', at the correct pen angle, then move it round the letter to see if seems the right size. Try another if it's too small. When you are sure, put some ink in the pen and make some nib-width markings between the lines. Note down how many there are.

4 Now you know enough to rule a few lines of your own and start copying – so next look at the shapes of the letters. Look especially at the shape of the O; this is important, because O usually governs the shape of several other letters. Is it rounded, oval, upright or sloped? Compare the O with other O-shaped letters

to see how they match; try copying a few.

5 Extensions: if it is lower-case text, how tall are the ascenders and descenders in proportion to the body height – the same again, half as much again, taller? (Take an average, remember the writer did not know his work was going to be studied so closely!)

6 Arches: in lower-case letters, the joining point, for example in the letter 'h', will usually be at the top (as in Foundational) or branching out from the bottom in a joined-up movement (as in Italic). The arch shape is often a critical pointer to the main characteristics of the script.

7 Speed: you will be slow when you first try copying it, but speed is important to note, as it does affect the appearance of letters. Clues to fast writing are: slope, shorter number of strokes per letter, no fancy serifs, exit stroke lifts up towards next letter. Clues to slow writing: lots of separate strokes per letter, any serif that takes extra work, upright, no unevenness, every letter separate.

8 So you now have seven points of reference, but you are probably short of a few letters, and will have to make them up. Use your knowledge of the letters you do have – for example, make a missing 'q' by studying how 'a', 'o', and 'p' work. Think of any alphabet as a matching ensemble – all the letters have to look as if they belong to the same collection.

First published in 2003 by ABBEYDALE PRESS,
an imprint of Bookmart Limited
Registered Number 2372865
Blaby Road, Wigston
Leicestershire LE18 4SE

© 2003 Bookmart Limited

Originally published by Bookmart Ltd as part of
Calligraphy Techniques in 2001

ISBN 1-86147-121-1

Printed in China